Big Cats
of the World

LEVEL **1** READER
READING · GRADES · K TO 1 · LEVEL

Written by Kathryn Knight
Illustrated by Edizioni Larus S.p.A.

bendon®

African Lion

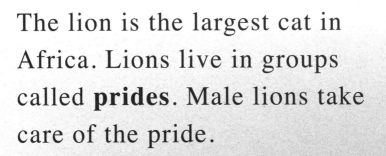

The lion is the largest cat in Africa. Lions live in groups called **prides**. Male lions take care of the pride.

READING LEVEL 1

GRADES K TO 1

BIG CATS
of the World

NATURE SERIES

When it is hot, lions rest
in the shade.

Baby lions are called **cubs**.
Cubs learn the rules of the
pride and how to hunt.

Cheetah

This graceful cat is the cheetah.
It is one of the fastest animals
in the world. It can run as fast
as a car!

The mother cheetah teaches
her cubs how to hunt.

Leopard

The leopard has spots to help it hide in the forest. Leopards live in Africa and southern Asia.

Leopards are strong and very good climbers. Sometimes they sit in a tree, looking for food.

Leopards hunt many different animals.

A black panther is really a leopard! Its spots are hard to see because its fur is dark.

Black leopards can hide in the shadows of the jungle.

Asian Lion

Asian lions are different from African lions. They have lighter fur and hunt smaller animals.

Bengal Tiger

Tigers have striped coats that help them hide in tall grass. The Bengal tiger is called the "royal tiger."

Bengal tiger cubs
stay with their mother until they
can live on their own.

The Bengal tiger is very strong.
It can hunt animals much
bigger than itself.

Snow Leopard

The snow leopard lives high in the mountains in Asia. It has a thick coat to keep it warm! Snow leopards are great hunters.

Clouded Leopard

Clouded leopards also live in Asia. They are smaller than snow leopards.

Clouded leopards live in forests. They are excellent tree climbers!

Siberian Tiger

The Siberian tiger is the largest cat in the world. It is a powerful and quick hunter.

The Siberian tiger likes to
live alone in the mountains.
It also hides in forests and
near rivers.

Lynx

The lynx is the largest wild cat in Europe. It has fur on the top of its ears and a short tail. It can climb trees and swim across rivers.

Canadian Lynx

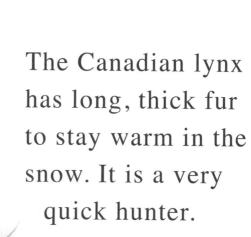

The Canadian lynx has long, thick fur to stay warm in the snow. It is a very quick hunter.

Canadian lynx cubs are cute balls of fluff!

Bobcat

The bobcat of North America
has a very loud cry. It hunts at
night and sleeps in the day.
Its favorite meal is a jackrabbit!

Ocelot

The ocelot (**ah**-suh-lot) is a small wild cat. It likes to hunt at night.

Ocelot cubs look and act just like kittens!

Jaguar

The jaguar is the largest cat of the
Americas. It lives in the rainforest.
It can climb trees and swim!

Mothers teach their
cubs to hunt. They
learn to find eggs,
catch fish, and chase
monkeys in the trees!

The jaguar hunts for deer,
fish, and reptiles.

Puma

Pumas live in cold mountains
and in hot deserts, too. Their fur
can be tan, red, or yellow-gray.

The puma is a strong hunter. It will
travel very far in search of food.

North American Puma (Cougar)

Pumas that live in North America are called cougars, mountain lions, or panthers. The cubs are born with spots. They lose their spots when they get older.

Cougar cubs are born
in a cave in the summer.
Their mother keeps
them safe.

A cougar can act like a really big
pet cat. But no matter how cute
they look, they are not pets. These
big cats are wild!